Dedicated to all the women that put in hard work and suffering to get us the vote. It was a long and arduous process.

# Feminism

<u>**Trapped In Negativity**</u>
She felt like a butterfly trapped in a cage
No matter how hard she tried to break the cage
All it did was push back
Cold metal brushing against her body
Slapping her with bruises
And tearing her wings inch by miserable inch
Pulling apart the very meaning of who she was
And what she did
She was meant to fly
But all she did was break
Her unique wings birthed by nature
Ripped at her shoulders
Until she no longer had a purpose
Resting against the floor
Bleeding and alone
No freedom
Just pain
Taken from her field of flowers
Too young

<u>**Admit It**</u>

If I was a question
Would you avoid me
Or deceive yourself with
False promises?
Would you answer me
Truthfully
Or give me away?
If I was an answer
Would you take me
Or lie and say it can't be
That way?
If I was a thought
Would you think me
At all?
If I was …

## Rain Goddess

She danced in the mist of grey
Her body swaying gently
Like a leaf drifting in the breeze
Her arms elegantly moving away from her sides
As her feet moved to steps only she could see
To a song only she could hear
She couldn't see past the smoke surrounding her
Body
Encasing her in a prison
In a bubble all her own
She was a raindrop
A single tear stuffed in a cloud of millions
Nature in its purest form
Mixing with the mud and sinking
Into the roots of a flower
Flowing into the cold dark body of another
And stretching it taller
Helping it to reach the sun
To grow
Giving yet never given too
Not allowed to become more
Then the purpose it was given
Not able to grow
Too warm to freeze the veins of another
Yet, not too timid to exist in the heat
Of the sun
Everyone thought she was someone else

So she convinced herself
She was only the nurture
Without a mind to think for itself
And so she cried
Falling down
Down
Down
Her cheek
The tear
Of the sky
And the woe
Of man
Like a storm
On a cloudy day
Dance
Drip
Dance
Drop
The woman in the raindrop

# **<u>Their Twisted Feminism</u>**

Twist the ring around your finger
Diamonds shining in the spotlight of the sun
As you smile to your neighbors
But laugh to yourself
Why did he love you
When all he wanted to do
was screw

Twist the veil around your head
White shining in the spotlight of the sun
As you smile to your fiance
But laugh to yourself
Why did you love him
As he made your bigger dreams dim

Twist the child around your body
Eyes shining innocently in the spotlight of the sun
As you smile to your child
But laugh to yourself
Why did you let this happen
As your happiness began to blacken

Marry me
With a ring so sweet
Take my poor virginity
Never frown and never grumble
Don't forget not to mumble
Whisper gently, whisper sweet
And remember when we did meet
Pop out kids

One, two, three
Do not worry, just agree
The woe of women doesn't matter
Cut the talk, cut the chatter
Diamonds buy the beauty mine
But when we wish for more, no time
Waste my life, waste my body
Whip me until I'm melancholy
Test me, cheat me, sometimes beat me

Because I am nothing without you




## Feminism

How can one word be so
Twisted
So shaken
So stirred
In a tumbled up
Rumbled up way
That being associated
With a single word
Is a bad thing
You treat the word
As unequal
As you treat the women

# Important Causes

## <u>Fedrick Douglas Says "No Votes For Women"</u>

Poison, soak between my teeth

Find my throat quickly and hug it

Like a mother would a child

Flow within my blood and fill me

Until I am no longer hungry

Teach my stomach harshness

And toss illegitimate acid

From deep within my body out

Upon the ground where it belongs

Work like my brain and

Make me learn nonsensical intelligence

Before my clasped hands do what I might regret

Replace the pen in my hand

And make me whole

Then never leave me

For you are a sweet perfume

Compared to the anger flowing through me

## **<u>Ghost in Divorce</u>**

You speak too much
But you say very little
With words of harshness and hate
I speak too little
Yet think too much
With thoughts of anger and pain

Try to live within my shoes
If even for a day
For I have tried
To live your life
For many more than you may

## <u>Steal My Sides</u>
Take your deceitful ways
And drive my hand towards my mouth
Taping it firmly shut
No words for the woman, you say

Lead my logic away to the biggest, brightest tower
Lock it away
So I think very little
No thinking for teens, you say

Take my anxiety and chain it to morality
As my passion simmers quickly
Make me fear who I may be
Fear for the sensitive soul, you say

Let my creativity
Sit all alone
Stupidly scratching down sentences
For one personality is struck down quickly
When no sense is constructed

<u>**To Daughter -Elizabeth Cady Stanton**</u>

My flower, you are no more delicate than
The thorns on your side
Sticking to the hands of the less fortunate
You are soft, yet your roots show strength
So small, yet easily seen with your colorful
Statement spoken so sassily
Do not let them break you
Overly sensitive you are not
Your opinion is yours
Let yourself blush brilliant red
As anger opens upon your cheeks
Banging against your broken brain

You matter my child

Young enough to see
Young enough to think
Yet never enough to him
So don't try to please him
He is just a weed

## Splitting of Organizations

We cross through the same door
With minds attached
Yet always leave to the same spot
Through separate doors
You leave me
Yet we both go north
Strange friend
Why do we always part
Yet go in the same direction?
Who are you to say goodbye when
We are a few feet apart?
I do not know you
We are strangers

## Elizabeth & Susan: Minds Like No Other

Why do we bend only to break
To bring those that we love happiness?
Why do we breathe to save the souls of the lost?
Why is family just a temporary definition?
And friends forever the same?

## Women Working

My delicate hands pounded as callouses pulsed
Underneath my skin
And my sweat ran rampant upon my forehead
In the pants that were a few sizes too big
Strong woman
Building the weapons
For the future
To bring hope to all that were stuck
In another endless war
Another cog in the murder machine
Yet doing the jobs we could have only wished to
have

My delicate hands pounded as callouses faded
Underneath my skin
And my sweat dried against my forehead
In the skirt that was a few sizes too small
Strong woman
Trading weaponry
For a typewriter
To bring hopelessness to all that were stuck
In another endless war
Another cog in the sex machine
Doing the jobs that were too brainless
For the poor little men

You said I shouldn't want trouble

That I'm the girl in the bubble
But I was more than the box
You set me in
Tools of my trade
Paint tears
Across my eyes

<u>**Feminine Mystique**</u>
You do your little dance
Every move perfectly formulated
As the spotlight shines on only you
Spinning your body wildly until you
Are nothing but a blur of color
No longer human as you twist right
And leap left
This was supposed to be our show
With our names shining high for all to see
But instead you bruised my bones
And run away from me with no intention
Of returning
Little boy blue cries pretend tears
And miss sunshine falls to let in the moon
As the earth slowly turns a rotation
This is not your little show
To fly and flutter
And I was not your pawn to move
To your pleasing
This is not your show
Not your stage
And not your time to shine
So back off
And let me find
My own dance
Without you

## Stanton's Women's Bible

The juice dribbled down her chin
Sticking to the skin as she took a bite
Her red lips painted as blood red
As the sin she had committed
And her hair shamefully draped over her
Bouncing breasts to cover the body
She had found to be evil

Her name meaning
The breath of life
Yet never living in history as the person
She was meant to be
Bible breaker, sin taker, baby maker
Yet nothing more
Just the Eve to his Adam
And the temptation that wreaked havoc
By opening her perfect lips
To speak with the body she had been gifted

No one saw past what she had done
She was defined by her mistake
No one focused on the fact
That her body was formed by a piece of his
Created as equals

No one focused on the fact
That she had helped name the world around them

Able to think

No one focused on the fact
That she had been tempted by the devil first
Fighting feistily with logic
Not giving in so easily

No one focused on the fact that she was forced into
a marriage
No choice to be who she wanted to be
Literally made for him
Yet wanting to be someone more

No one focused on the fact that maybe
She loved her curves
And her breasts
And her vagina
And her hips
But she felt like she would be shamed
If she didn't cover herself up
Because her husband was ashamed of his body

You are my sweetest downfall
Bittersweet woe of a woman

The tears welled in her eyes
Sticking to her skin as he banished her
Her arms wrapped around

The body she had denied
Her hair wrapped around the curves
She had found to be evil

Her name meaning
Beautiful
Yet never living in history as the person
She was meant to be
Man hater, sin creator, title breaker
Yet nothing more
The queen banished in a story
About the king's second wife
Just the woman who disobeyed
By opening her perfect lips
To deny him the perfect body she had been gifted

No one saw past what she had done
She was defined by her mistake
No one focused on the fact
That she had denied him her body
Woman with brains and beauty

No one focused on the fact
That her self-respect meant more than a kingdom
Woman with high character

No one focused on the fact
That she was not tricked by her husband

Not giving in so easily

No one focused on the fact that
She was forced into a lifestyle
No choice to be who she wanted to be
Literally taught to be for him
Yet wanting to be someone more

No one focused on the fact that maybe
She loved her brain
And her intelligence
And her self respect
And her personality
And she felt like she deserved more
Then to be treated like a common slut
Because her husband was drunk and stupid

You are my sweetest downfall
Bittersweet woe of a woman

The youth fell from her weary eyes
Pain stuck to her skin as her childhood was stolen
The son of christ sucking on her breast
As she fed the son with her teenage body
Her hair stuck to her tired body
As she tried to serve her God

Her name meaning

Wished for child
Yet never living in history as the person
She should have been
Sin hater, lord creator, title taker
Yet nothing more
Just the virgin who birthed christ
By opening her perfect lips
To give him entrance into the world

No one saw past what she had done
She was defined by her virginity and motherhood
No one focused on the fact
That she had been a child herself
Birthing and caring for a child not her own

No one focused on the fact
That she was targeted because she was a virgin
Like that was a good thing

No one focused on the fact
That she just went along with it
Because she had no other choice

No one focused on the fact that
She was forced to be a mother
No choice to be who she wanted to be
Literally forced to be someone
Yet wanting to be someone more

No one focused on the fact that maybe
She wanted to be seen for more than her body
And her sexuality
And her one single achievement
By allowing a man to impregnate her
At such a young age and be the mother
She should never have become
She felt like she deserved more
Then to be treated like a baby carrier

You are my sweetest downfall
Bittersweet woe of a woman

Twisted, turned, and written out of history
Lives nothing more than an unwanted mystery
Because no one wanted
To hear of a woman's misery

The dangers of a single story

# **<u>Alice Paul Picketing & Strike</u>**

Your mouth screams at me
Breath as rancid as rotting fish
Streaked against the bottom of a garbage bag
Spewing against my face
And leaving angry wet sludge against my cheek

You tell me I am "Obstructing traffic"
That my weak body that you use to wipe
Your boots beneath without remorse
Until I'm broken and bloody
Is such a roadblock that I need to leave

Well I am more than fragile
And I am more than weak
So run me over if you dare

Take away my right to speak my mind
Tear down my body
Rip my arms from their sockets
As you stuff them into chains
Tear my feet off at the knees
As you beg me to submit
And tear the skin from my throat
As you shove food down my
Starved stomach
Demanding I eat when you want me to

Does it get your blood boiling
When we push back at you
Painting your ugly with what
You assumed would be our sweet

Does it make you see red
When we get in the way
Trying to fight for our rights
That you have denied so easily

Does it get in your head
That we are human too
And that we can speak just
The way you do

Good

# Important
# People & Quotes

**"Women help to mold the character of a
country and determine its destiny."
-Sojourner Truth**

She takes her delicate hands painted grey and dips
Them in the cold clay of the earth
Holding it in her palm as she hums softly to herself
Hidden behind a veil of misconceptions as she
Twists her fingers in an intricate design
Cupping the foundation of the planet as she creates
A template from memory
Like a wizard spinning a spell and a maiden lost in
A cage
She twists until her hands ache and her back
Protests
Dirt stuck beneath her nails
And sweat balancing delicately across her brows
Two hundred and eighty days until it hardens
Stuck against her palm and sucking her blood dry
Pouring laughter and kindness into its every surface
And patience into its every crack
Washing away her tears from the pain and suffering
She was meant to stuff beneath a box
Locked within her chest
As she dances through the numbness
And submissively concedes
Wrapping layers of her bubble wrap around her
Creation

And stapling her eyes wide as she watches her
Creation suck her dry
Waiting for the help that would never come
Eighteen years and one month until she can breathe
Again
Yet setting herself back like a time machine
As she weaves character into every building block
That builds
The country she stands her weary feet upon
Dreaming of a destiny greater than what she had
Been given
Strong woman weeps for her child
As she hides in a cage
Of her other half
Waiting for the day
She would be freed

**"Her kingdom is not over physical forces.
Not by might, nor by power can she prevail
… In the reign of moral ideas, she is easily
queen." -Anna Julia Cooper**

She sat kneeling down on the beach
Her golden hair stained with dirt
And her scarred hands holding her scorched and
Tattered dress
Watching as the ash fell around her like
Impure snow
Burying the castle caged in a ring of fire

A single paper crown sinking into the sea
As her glass heart shattered, disintegrating like dust

She had made it out

But she was never the same

Blue mixing with red against the mirror of her soul
Cuts framing her face like a picture
And burns painting her skin like a rainbow painting
The sky

They had built her wall too high
Chaining her to a wall and sinking needles
Deep into her perfect skin to keep her submissive

Trapping her as they built the walls around her
Until she could no longer see the light
Her voice drained dry from the screams
That no one had ever heard
Alone in the deep, dark, depths of her mind
Sinking underwater and submerged as she fought
Trying to stay afloat in the dark pit of the ocean

No one had come to save her
No knight in shining armor
No king that had pledged their life
But she didn't need it
She was strong all her own

All she needed was to be seen
All she wanted was to be herself
All she is is a woman trapped by her body
All she ever was is compromised
All she finds
Is pain, trapped within her mind

**"So close is the bond between man and woman that you cannot raise one without lifting the other." -Frances Harper**

Auras twisted together as one
Bend in a helix of unknown power
Entwined Equals in a land where
Equality can not exist
Unbalanced and unfair
As one breaks free from the other
Floating higher

Two auras twisting like wire
Bending in a helix of unknown power
Entwined equals
Where equality can not exist
Unbalanced and unfair

One tries to fly away
And the other falls further down
Watching close
The other wants to as well
But it is a lie
In the land of inequalities

I'll believe it all
There's nothing I won't understand
I'll believe it all
I won't let go of your hand
They had promised each other forever
They had sworn love for all eternity

But one of them had been lying
In a land of inequalities

One more or one less
Nobody's worried
When one rises further
Lost to the sky
And one is broken
Laying on the dirty ground
Power of the powerless
The only hope
To break the spell
And fix them both
In a land of
Inequalities

Two auras twisting like wire
Say they're always gonna stay together
But one's never going to let go of the power
He says that he will
But he's just a liar

**"He has denied her the facilities for obtaining a thorough education." -Stanton, Declaration of Sentiments**

You sit behind me in class
Twirling my curls in your hand
And cutting my braids from my head at the root
Leaning over my shoulder
As your greedy eyes take in
What my sore, aching hand had created
Copycat, copycat steal my words divine
Copycat, copycat memories of mine
Pulling my head from my shoulders
And draining the words from my lips
With a knife
And a pen

You laugh loudly, tearing my work in two
As you paint your name in blue
Waving it proudly in the air
Waiting for the big red A
To appear with a magic twist of the teacher's wand
Copycat, copycat steal my words divine
Copycat, copycat memories of mine
Tearing off my skull as you prick me with pins
To fill your ink like you filled my eyes
With tears

Big mighty principal slaps my wrist
With a ruler until I'm bruised and bloodied
Chaining my hands with metal
Until my fingers turn purple
And slapping my eyes with tape
Until I am blind to all the world
My hot breath the only noise in my dead ears
As you wipe my mind from thinking
And shut my lips from speaking
Telling me all the while
That I was just to look at
Copycat, copycat steal my words divine
Copycat, copycat memories of mine

You stole my knowledge
Before I could grow
You push me to the
 G
   R
     O
       U
         N
           D
Not expecting me to get back up again
Twisting my arm around my back
Until my skin cracks
Beneath your brutish hands

                         As they tear my arms in two
                    Your hot breath stopping my screams
                    As you whisper threats into my ears


Growling deep
    And low


In a voice that has me frozen


You tell me I should be handled with care
Yet all you do is take me in your hands
And tear me down
Until I am nothing but a blanket of skin draped
Over bruised and broken bones like a band aid


                              You tell me I should be loved
                    Yet all you do is teach my blue heart hate
                              I am more than what you give me
                    And I deserve more than what you give me
                                             Day after day


All the wives and all the mothers know
That love is foreign in our world
Where you push your foot against us
Keeping us to the floor
And sweeping the dust from your shoe as you
Rub our bodies against the carpet

Collecting mud and dirt and grim


You all call us beautiful
You all call us delicate
But what is so delicate about being a doormat?

**"Taught to regard marriage as the one thing needful … win the attentions of men, by their external charms." -Sarah Grimke**

I can't be everything if I am yours
You have the other half of me
Just like when the sun falls
And takes with it, the light
You take a piece of me
And bring me to a calming night

But that light is sent back by being
Reflected off of the moon and
Brings us light in the darkness
You are my sun, my moon, my torch
Anywhere there is darkness
You shine through and bring light
Into my life

I concede that even the darkness has light
But light is nothing without
The calm beauty of its creation
You are the beauty that fills my light
You are the molecules
And particles that bind together
Bending my light
Where it needs to shine brightest
You change the direction

Of where I need to go
You are my rainbow, my stars, and my sunset
You take me where I need to be

But then you tear me apart
Stomping my other half to the dirt
And wiping your brow with my heart
Until my soul is flickering
Like a half-dead lighting bug
In a sea of a summer storm
And as I lay there thinking
With my brain once more
I see that was how it really
Always had been
Obvious to all but me

Some mistakes get made
My mistake had been trusting you
And falling so far into your eyes
That I lost sight of my own
Turning off my head with
The engagement ring choking my hand

But that's alright, that's okay
Right? Isn't it?
As I let you be the person that
Society has defined within my mind
As you push me into a box

And force me to be the womb
Until I fall into the grave
But it's all alright
It's all okay. Won't it be?


Some people fall in love with the wrong person
Really it's foolish
To have fallen in love with any man
But you cannot think at all
When the world spins against you
And tries everything it can
To keep you submerged
Beneath layers of ocean
Struggling to breathe
Surrounded by sea


You can think that you're in love
When you're really just in pain
Stuck in an endless cycle of living
Where women were nothing but a doll
Stuck on a string dancing
You should have seen the signs
Should have seen them flashing red
Yet all you saw was the big black
Do not pass go


Well if you only saw me now

This is Karma right here honey
I can stop and help you if you want nice and sweet
But I can flip like a switch just as easily
In the end it's better for me

That's the moral of the story babe

Even if I was never able to tell you

**"He has compelled her to submit to laws, in
the formation of which she had no voice."
-Stanton, Declaration of Sentiments**

I believe that one day we will be strong
That the tape that once bound our mouths will break
And the people who muted us
Will mute us no longer
I believe that one day we will be independent
That we won't follow others like sheep
And we will think for ourselves as people
I believe that one day we will be peaceful
That we will learn that
Violence doesn't end violence
And hate doesn't end hate, it extends it
I believe that one day this world will be beautiful
That the people on this measly planet
Will learn to communicate
To love everyone no matter who they are inside
To help anyone no matter how different
To end all of this foolishness and actually make a
Change instead of walking around like blind mice
Right now this world has seemed to lose its shine
The shine that had brought joy to all that had seen it
We ruined that shine, that beauty that mother nature
Had brought so graciously to us
The majestic beasts have been locked in cages
The oceans have become wastelands

And we have become monsters
We are constantly trying to evolve, to become better
Yet we are shaming people because they
Are more evolved then us
Because they understand love better than us
Because they are better than us
And people hate that
So they ridicule them
And hate them, And hurt them
And try to make them 'better'
When really, 'better' is actually worse
Maybe just maybe those muters, those people that
Hate simply because they have no opinion of their
Own, those people
That stuck the tape on our mouths and silenced us
Maybe they are the sickness in this world
The disease that is draining America dry
Killing every living thing on this planet
Well, I have something to say to you, disease
I don't care if you yell at me, or ridicule me
Or hate me
I don't care if you scream it at the top of your lungs
My voice WILL be heard
For every person ever pushed down
For being who they are
Every human being that has ever been hated
For being different
To you diseased minds

I am sick of you
I am sick of your hate
And I am sick of you acting like you know best
Your life is not my life
Your choices are not my choices
I am my own person
They are their own person and
You will treat them as such
They are just like you
You have a heart, emotions
And so do they
Do not try and break an unbreakable
Because they are so much than you could ever be
You are half the human they are
And maybe one day you'll be better
But until then you can suck it up
You can keep your opinions to yourself
And you can stop acting like you are some type of
God that knows how to live my life
Their life
I believe that one day this damn earth can change
It just takes love and understanding to get there
So make it happen

**"Fashionable women regard themselves and are regarded by men, as pretty toys or as mere instruments of pleasure." -Sarah Grimke**

All you want to do is pluck my strings
And then leave me in a home all alone
Expecting me to smile and flutter
Frozen like a doll as I clean and cook

Stuck in a world where my imperfections
Are nothing but a fantasy
And my mind is forever empty

Wrap your hands around my throat
Until I beg
Scratching at your skin for money
And the air to breathe

Paint me like a picture
And show me what you see
Let me flutter my eyes
And sing with pretty lips soaked in honey
Let me be who you need me to be

Take me where I need to go
And let me be your perfect dolly
Pretending to be what nature created

Sewing crimson buttons on eyes
And brown hair of thick yarn
Naked to the world around me

    Drawing clothes on with sharpie
    And shoes on with glitter
    An illusion to the world around me

        Yet I was empty
        For I needed a brain
        And all I had was stuffing

## <u>Too Pretty</u>

Scars cut a trail down her bleeding mouth
Etching deep-rooted weeds into her skin
And entwining the forbidden memories of a world
Where she need not fight for her right to be known
Her own blood wrapping around her
Like a bed of satin
Resting against her skin
As her ragged breath protested
Begging to scream out yet held back
Trapped deep within her throat and
Held back by her own body
At war with herself and the people that called her
Love
Torn by society and tortured with a smile
Tainted by the sweet nothings
That they said in her ear
As they waved her off like a fly
Saying there was no need to worry her little head
Or dirty her clean porcelain nails
Even when she protested
That her mind always thought
And her hands were already dirty from the get-go
Stained by their words
As they clawed their way to the top
To protect their precious egos
From taking a fall
Take but never give

Talk but never listen
Twirling in circles as she flutters her eyelashes
Held up by the ear and screamed at
As she gave her all
But never took
Listening as their words swirled around her
But never spoke
Proper, petite, perfect
Woman

## Used Beyond Recognition

You take my body and put me on the bed
Spreading me as far as I can go as you take
Everything you needed from me
Pulling my legs and clawing at my skin
Before leaving me stranded at home to protect
The innocent eyes that call me mother

You tell me you love me
And kiss me sweetly
Whispering gently against my lips
Telling me that I am your forever
Pulling a cloth around my eyes
And blinding me with a veil of misconceptions
Anything to distract my delicate heart
From the motives that you think I can't see
Not realizing that your every lie was masked behind
The truth that you screamed for all to hear
Providing me with everything I need

I know that you are using me
That I am nothing more than your doll
That you bend me
Break me
And take me
All in the name of society

I try to fight back

To scream and shout
But no one listens

So

Use me
Use me
Use me

I know that it is too easy to get me to do what you
ask
But I would bite back easily
If anyone was willing to listen to me

I know that you don't need me
But you do it anyways

So

Use me
Use me
Use me

Until I can't be used anymore

## Wonder Woman

Break the chains that bind my wrist
Like the weight around my heart
Stomping down on all that ails me
As I force a lasso around their throats
Pulling them down on their knees
Cleaning the floor that they
Had made dirty with their shoes
Power is as power does
You, good gentlemen,
Have been anything but gentle
You have pushed needles into my tongue
And you have forced me into a man-made handcuff
Burning my "delicate" skin with rough, worn rope
As you laughed in my face and called me crazy
Well no more
I am more than just a woman
But you treat me like your toy
And you wonder why I try to break free?
Wonder no more
It is time you see all of me

## **Love Should Be**

Love should be earned not expected or taken
Choices create the very foundation
Of what is right and what is wrong
In a world where it takes so long
To give what should be given

When love turns into the only rulebook
And strong choices leave the world shook
As half the population denies the definition
To subtract their ego and make the addition
Of women into the law

Nobody wins in the chess game of life
As women struggle through their strife
To win the equality they deserve
In a world where morals of men have curved
In a twisted sort of manner

Prim and proper and stapled tongues
As they stayed in the homes where children sprung
From a womb attached to a denied sort of mind
And men did claim that the vote was defined
As only for their strong heads

Women toss and women turn
Always obedient but always burned
As men took the love women wanted

And told them they had already got it, taunted
Because they only needed children

Love should be earned not expected or taken
Choices create the very foundation
Of where women back then had gone
In a world where they did play the pawn
To give what the men had wanted

## <u>Follow The Leader</u>

Tell me who you think you are
To tell me that my hands smooth and pure
Are meant to twist and turn until they fall
Dead to the floor
Withering with blood red skin
Sheding to reveal a strong white bone

Tell me who you think you are
To tell me that my eyes so tired and crying
Should dance around the room
Until they rip themselves from my sockets
And slip from my hands
Blinded to my own life and instead seeing yours

Tell me who you think you are
To tell me that my different feet, broken already
Should move until they break again and form
Newer and brighter souls
White poking out from torn, tattered skin
Like wings extending beyond imagination

Tell me who you think you are with words so malice
To tell me what I should do and what I should become
When you are no more than a leader of the past
Trying to relive past glories

# Sugar, Spice, And Nothing Nice

I stand in a field of tulips
Frozen as they circle me like ravens hunting mice
Listening as their stomachs growl
Begging for more
They tear at my body, cutting down to the bone
Peeling me away until I am bare
Satisfying their own hunger
They take the frosting sitting in my chest
Sugar and honey falling from my lips
Like a broken faucet, forever flowing
I hear them whisper
Telling me I am just another lollipop
To break beneath their teeth
Discarding the essential cake
I hide within
Deep in the hidden caverns of the trash
Underneath toenail clippings
And rotten food poisoned by time
It's all my fault
All my bad
Because I taste so good
Yet, if I called them meat
And bit them to the bone
I would be hated just as much
There is no winning
In the world of a woman
I am a trickster, a trap

A spider weaving my web of manipulation
I am just a piece of cake
Taunting, tempting
Begging for you
To take a bite

<u>**Soap**</u>
I am trapped in a bubble
Pushing and pulling
But never once able to break free
From the bubble that surrounds me

The air gets thinner
As I try to breathe
Gasping for air as nothing
But toxic soap fills my lungs

I fell to the floor holding my neck
As I tried to scream out for air
But all I could taste was the soap
Shaping with the water within me as bubbles
Fell from my blue lips

I could feel it coming up my throat
Wishing I had never said a word
Yet too far gone to make amends
With the gods up above

I was tired of being careful
I was tired of being gentle
So I had let my faucet overflow
Speaking my opinions
Even if I knew
It would get me into trouble

I am trapped in my bubble
Pushing and pulling to leave

The trap that surrounds me
Leaving me in misery
But never once able to break free
From the bubble that surrounds me

So I guess I'm going to wash my mouth out with soap

# Sun & Moon

The sun burns, her fire-orange dress
The epitome of beauty and her copper hair
Blazing like a halo around her head
Her crimson lips turned up in a curious smirk
She was seen as a lion
The fiercest ruler in all the land
Turning smiles into frowns and cold into hot t
The second she snaps
Her dark brown eyes your way
They call her Nova, for she burns brighter than all

The moon shines, her glittering grey gown
The epitome of perfection and her silky, calm hair
Like Ocean waves surrounding her head
Her lips turned up into a serene smile
She was seen as a owl
The kindest and wisest ruler in all the land
Turning frowns into smiles and hot into cold the
Second she brings her diamond blue eyes
To meet yours
They call her Selene
For she is quite simply, the moon

What people do not realize
As they stare upon the women of the world
Is that the lion is just protective
Making sure her cubs are safe

For Nova was a fair ruler, just in all her rules
But the owl that hunts in the night
Preying on the week is not just at all
Selene was coincided
Ruined by her beauty
Condemning her people
To live their lives as stars in the sky
We are people ruled by both
Never able to see the full picture
And so I tell you now
Instead of just looking at one piece of the puzzle
Look further, and see the whole picture
Luna is forever favored
As the favorite of the women
And Nova the hated of the two
Do not judge a girl by the clothes she wears
The way her hair surrounds her head
The color of her aura
Judge a girl by the personality she has
And only by that

# Present Feminism

# America The Brave

The woman with the rose and the raven hair
Whispers sweet truth
Hidden only by a perfume of thick nature
A poison so addicting yet so unnatural to the world
And a woman never once believed
For who could believe an innocent child
Who hasn't lived
Just a ghost
Sinking, falling, lost in her own mind

She whispers to me at night
Telling me stories
Weaving my dreams

The woman with the rose and
The raven hair tells me sweet truth
"America the brave" she says,
Is a land of regrets
A land where the brave are idiots
That speak their nasty words
To those that are worse off than themselves
A land where hate is common
And no one blinks an eye
A land where rich is power
Where greed buys a person

The woman with the rose and the raven hair
explains to me the sweet truth
"America the free" she says,
Is a land of chained drones
A land where every unique thought
Is no longer unique
A land where every idea
Is just an opinion
Of someone more powerful
A land where one is judged
For being truly different
Chained by society's laws

The woman with the rose and t
The raven hair
Screams at me the sweet truth
"America the beautiful" she says,
Is a land caked in cracking makeup
And dollar store perfume
A land where depression
And suicide rates have risen
To the highest they ever were
A land where words are
Always double-edged swords
That always hit their mark no matter what
A land where there is no hope
No trust
And where love

No longer exists

The woman with the rose and the raven hair
Hands me a single rose of sweet, sweet truth
Yet my ears ring
And my head spins from pain
As she whispers a single thought in my mind
Holding me close
"Long live America, they say,
yet we were never living to begin with."
I grasp the rose, tears falling from my ashy face
As blood seeps through my hands
Dripping down my skinny arms
And dropping to the floor like crimson tears

The girl with the bloody rose and the fire hair falls
Collapsing as black clothing chokes her body
Resting in a coffin of the purest of white
As she walks among the living
Her lips forever sealed

Dead to a world not worth living in

## **<u>Self-Defense</u>**

Go for the throat
Dig nails into skin
And peel away
To reveal the monster underneath
Kick where it counts
Make one become two
And use power
Where one might have none
Use the sword of
Wondrous words
And the shield of denial
Show them that violence
Extends violence
Because a woman is not a toy
To smile and be taken advantage of
A woman is
A weapon

## **You Made Me A Mess, But I'm Gonna Clean Up**

Why are the best things sour
To my unsuspecting mouth?
Why do I pucker my lips
When I should feel nothing but pleasure?
The wind slaps against my cheeks
And forbidden fruit drips down my lips
As you tell me who I should be
Well don't even try
I am gonna fly
Far away from you
And live my life
This is mine
And my heart will love who I please
Your sour will be my sweet
I just decided

# Never Signed Up

You say lines perfectly formulated
By a writer hidden behind a curtain
Trying to impress me with elaborate costumes
And stagings of delicate designs
But I don't care
There is a whole world around you
Yet you decide to stick yourself in a play
Hoping I wouldn't see behind your mask
Of hate and love mixing like oil and water
In a giant jar half in the dark
You offend me
We repeal like north and south
East and west
You act like just because I give you kindness
That suddenly it binds us like glue
But I never signed up for your drama club
I am not your queen to demand
Or your actress to direct
I am a one-woman play
Do not just assume that we were meant to be
When all you do is feed me a script
And repeat yourself again and again
Like a puppet
Take a bow
And wake up
It is never going to happen

# **<u>Strawberry Shortcake</u>**

You say the cruelest words
Painting my body like eggs
Boiled in blood and coated in rotting mud
Twisting my hair and tearing it from my scalp
As you laugh from the pedestal I built
From the gold my hands dug and the silver
I traded my mind for
You laugh at me, kicking me in a ditch
That I formed as a grave
Why do you look down at me
Yet your lips soaked in sugar tell me
That you love me
My flour
So delicate
Can never rise if you overwork it with
Poison and acid
You try to paint me with icing
But you follow your own directions
I am not your strawberry shortcake
To share with your friends
And critique so harshly
Love is not a mouth to feed
And I am not a silver spoon
To shove up your ass
I am a human
Beautifully created
And yes

I may be short
Not risen as tall as the rest of the desserts
You have run your sticky little hands across
But I have a lot more flavor
On the inside
That you don't give me credit for
Lick your fingers all you want
But I am a forbidden fruit
So spend your money
Elsewhere
Because I'm not here
For you

## Electing Men

A blonde-haired beauty
With eyes of crystal blue
And curves of delicate nature
Sits, pinning after all the wrong men
Wondering, brokenly, why none of them want to
put her together again
One feeds her lies
And two call her ugly
Yet all of them cut her go
Tossing her around
Until she is dizzy
Masking deception
Like only a playboy can
Play the game
And never win
For love has long since been lost
America the brave
America the beautiful
Masochist until the end
Hurt me
Break me
And never take me
For I am used to being torn

## **<u>Thorn in Your Side</u>**

You try to pretend like you love me
Like I am your everything
The rose
The queen
The princess
And you treat me as such
But then one thing doesn't go your way
One single thing that doesn't matter and you blow
your fuse
You treat me like dirt
Like a villain
Like I was the one that had hurt you
And just like that everything goes wrong
You tear me off my pedestal and rip me to shreds
with your vicious words and cruel attitude
You break my bones and kill my heart
Through it all I try to remain happy
I try not to say anything
To bite back my hateful remarks, when all I'm
really thinking is
Who made you the king?
What makes you think you can speak to me in such
a way?
I stop myself from reacting
From bowing
From complying
From calling you 'your majesty'

And I hold myself firm, a plastic mask over my face
As the emotions wander my brain, far from reach
All I've ever wanted was to make everyone happy,
but today I say no more
No more hate
No more torture
No more
I am not a punching bag to
Beat to get your aggression out
I am not a villain
Or a piece of dirt
I am a person
With feelings and a heart and thoughts of my own
You are not royalty
Not my king to rule me how you like
I am a rose, and you are the thorns
I am a queen, and you are my kingdom
I am a princess, and you are the dragon I've slain
You may push me off my pedestal,
But I put myself back on top
I don't need you with your words
Your aggression
I am me
And all I need is myself

<u>**Then/Now**</u>

I mix red with blue
Mixing pot of emotions
The love I once felt
Sinking
Quiet despair
As you promise me forever

My eyes, broken
Melting salt like candle wax
Drip down
Scarred cheek, burned
As you tell me that the crayons
Were meant for me
And that the permanent markers
Were only for the you

I create a picture
Swirl fears and dreams
Together as one
To create a world
Where 1 = 1
Instead of
Inequality

I mix black with blue
Mixing pot of emotions
The love I once felt
Dead
Screaming despair
As you promise me forever

But give me nothing but pain in return

I mix red with blue
Mixing pot of emotions
The love I once felt
Irrelevant
No despair
As I promise myself forever

My eyes, broken
Melting salt like candle wax
Drip down
Scarred cheek, burned
As I work to balance my crayons
And my permanent markers
Together on a shelf, expertly
Little sleep

I create a movie
Swirl hopes and wishes
Together as one
To create a world
Where I am free
Instead of
Just a confined me

I mix black with blue
Mixing pot of emotions
The love I once felt
Useless

No despair
As I promise myself forever

But give myself everything in return


## **<u>Rare</u>**
Her diamond eyes shined brightly
As he circled her hungrily
Seeing her worth
Yet not not seeing her for who she was
She was seen as prim
She was seen as perfect
With her golden locks curled
And her emerald dress straightened
Down to the smallest seem
Yet he never saw past her body
She was just another woman in a sea of million
Not recognized for just how
Rare
She was
For just how brilliant
she could be
She was money
Nothing more
And she made up for her insurmountable cost
With the body that cursed him by breathing.

## <u>Warmth of Another Kind</u>

Her arms wrap around the sun
A distant moon that watches over all
She is strong and independent
And she whispers stories into the clouds
Wrapping them in delicate bows

Her smile warms the ground
A ray of sun that warms the earth
She is strong and independent
And she sends her stories to the oceans for all to
consume
Wrapping them in letters of the grandest thanks

Her eyes hold both light and dark
A distant star shining for all to see
She is strong and independent
And she holds her stories in her very shine
Wrapping them in a shine unlike any other
Women of the earth